ideals®
CHRISTMAS

Christmas comes softly to the waiting heart,
In candle's glow and star and ringing bell.
Across the snow, glad welcome lights the way
To hearth and home where
joy and laughter dwell.
—CAROL BESSENT HAYMAN

IDEALS PUBLICATIONS

NASHVILLE, TENNESSEE

Last-Minute Shopper

Lolita Pinney

Do your Christmas shopping early
Is advice I would ignore—
Let who will do autumn shopping—
I love late shopping more!

Just to see the stores a-twinkle
In their holiday array,
And to watch a child in Toyland
As he stops to dream and play,

Then to hear the sidewalk Santas
With their kettles and brass bells
Stirs one's heart to thoughts of sharing
As it whispers, "All is well!"

To choose a gift for someone
With some stardust in your eyes
Makes you eager for its giving,
For it's new—and a surprise!

Merry greetings are contagious
As you elbow through the throng;
Starry snowflakes stud your footsteps
As the wind blows clean and strong.

Let who will do autumn shopping
On a sunny autumn day—
But for me last-minute buying
Is the only joyful way!

The Last-Minute Rush
Harriet Whipple

We begin to think of Christmas
Around Thanksgiving Day
And make our lists, and purchase cards,
But it still seems far away.
Quite leisurely, we look for gifts
Each time we're in a store
To be sure last-minute shopping
Shan't besiege us as before.

Then suddenly we realize
It's but two short weeks away,
And we join the crowds out shopping
With no time left to delay.
We address cards and mail them
While regretting so much haste,
Wrap packages to hide or mail—
Not a moment can we waste.

We put candles in the windows,
Hang the sprig of mistletoe;
The holly wreath goes on the door
With its perky scarlet bow.
Then the turkey must be ordered,
And the goodies must we buy.
Cranberry sauce should soon be made,
And the mince and pumpkin pie.

There are programs needing costumes,
And some treats for parties too;
And driving kids to these affairs
Is a task we'll have to do.
That same last-minute rush again—
But somehow we get it done;
And, after all, it's Christmastime,
And the rush is rather fun!

For Christmas
Rachel Field

Now not a window small or big
But wears a wreath or holly sprig;
Nor any shop too poor to show
Its spray of pine or mistletoe.
Now city airs are spicy-sweet
With Christmas trees along each street,
Green spruce and fir whose boughs
     will hold
Their tinseled balls and fruits of gold.
Now postmen pass in threes and fours
Like bent, blue-coated Santa Claus.
Now people hurry to and fro
With little girls and boys
     in tow,
And not a child but keeps
     some trace
Of Christmas secrets in
     his face.

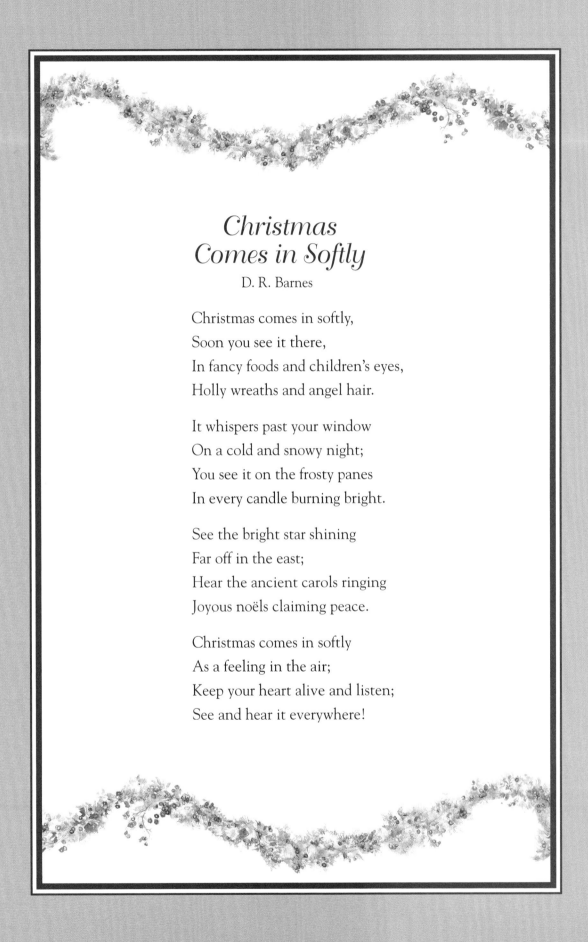

Christmas Comes in Softly

D. R. Barnes

Christmas comes in softly,
Soon you see it there,
In fancy foods and children's eyes,
Holly wreaths and angel hair.

It whispers past your window
On a cold and snowy night;
You see it on the frosty panes
In every candle burning bright.

See the bright star shining
Far off in the east;
Hear the ancient carols ringing
Joyous noëls claiming peace.

Christmas comes in softly
As a feeling in the air;
Keep your heart alive and listen;
See and hear it everywhere!

Photograph by Jessie Walker

Christmas Comes
to Our House

Nora M. Bozeman

Christmas comes to our house
And weaves her magic there,
She's trimmed the trees with tinsel shine
And wears white angel hair.

Wreaths and ribbons and holly,
Garlands of berries and pine,
Frosted windows and candleglow
In a Christmas-card design.

Christmas comes to our house
Decked in pageantry,
And when she sings her joyful songs—
That's Christmastime to me.

December

John Clare

As tho' the homestead trees were drest,
In lieu of snow, with dancing leaves,
As tho' the sun-dried martin's nest,
Instead of icicles, hung the eaves,
The children hail the happy day—
As if the snow were April's grass,
And pleas'd, as 'neath the warmth of May,
Sport o'er the water froze to glass.

Now is the season of the holly and the mistletoe; the days are come in which we hang our rooms with the sober green of December and feel it summer in our hearts.
—THE SATURDAY EVENING POST, DECEMBER 29, 1866

A snowy day at the Mountain Top Inn in Chittenden, Vermont. Photograph by William H. Johnson

Choose wisely, then, each ornament
And frosted tinsel skein
For branches that have worn jewels
Of gleaming mountain rain.
—ELIZABETH-ELLAN LONG

The Family Will Come

Fritz Peters

Deep in the winter night, the family will come one by one, carrying great and small boxes, brilliant in all colors, ribboned in red and green, silver and gold, bright blue, placing them under me with the hands of their hearts; until all around me they are piled high, climbing up into my branches, spilling over onto the floor about me. In the early morning, with all my candles burning and all my brilliant colors standing out and twinkling in their light, the children, in their pajamas and woolen slippers, rub their sleeping eyes and stare at me in amazement. The mother, with her hair hanging down her back, smiles and glances here and there, and the father looks up and down at me, quiet and pleased . . . for I am the Christmas tree.

WHAT A FOREST of brilliantly bedecked evergreen would be visible were all the firs that are to be laden and lighted this year brought together; and what a story that forest would tell of busy hands and buzzing consultations; of secrets it was hard to keep; of restless expectations and wistful looks; of the joy of givers and the gladness of receivers; of, in a word, the merry sympathy of warm affection.

—*The Saturday Evening Post*, December 28, 1867

Our Christmas Tree
Wendell Berry

Our Christmas tree is
not electrified, is not
covered with little lights
calling attention
    to themselves
(we have had enough
of little lights calling attention
to themselves). Our tree
is a cedar cut here, one
of the fragrances of our place,
hung with painted cones
and paper stars folded
long ago to praise our Tree,
Christ come into the world.

My Mother's Christmas Tree
Billy C. Clark

She did not want a cedar tree—
Claimed it was not Christmasy
Enough—and so we searched to find
With symmetry a native pine;
Then down the slope through fallen snow
We stopped to gather mistletoe
And bittersweet lit up at night
Not by bulbs but soft moonlight.
She shunned electricity
Or ornaments that one could see
Were made by man and then store-bought
Instead of being nature wrought,
Where the Spirit was more apt to stay
With us, on this, a Christmas Day.

Photograph by Jessie Walker

December

Aileen Fisher

I like days
with a snow-white collar,
and nights when the moon
is a silver dollar;
and hills are filled
with eiderdown stuffing,
and your breath makes smoke
like an engine puffing.

I like days
when feathers are snowing,
and all the eaves
have petticoats showing;
and the air is cold,
and the wires are humming,
but you feel all warm . . .
with Christmas coming!

O the snow, the beautiful snow,
Filling the sky and the earth below.
Over the housetops, over the street,
Over the heads of the people you meet,
Dancing,
Flirting,
Skimming along,
Beautiful snow, it can do nothing wrong.
— J. W. WATSON

Tongass National Forest, Arkansas.
Photograph by Carr Clifton

White Christmas

Susan Hill

It wouldn't be a white Christmas. That's what they told me. There hadn't been one for years.

I didn't say anything. But I knew.

Of course, there always used to be—so the old people in the village say.

Summers were long and hot, and it always snowed at Christmas.

That's how they remember it. And the men who built our village church must have gone through some bad times too, with ice and snow for months on end.

The weather was a lot different then, they say. I sometimes think of them, hauling the great blocks of stone and chiseling them into shape, up on the tower in the teeth of a blizzard, with blue hands and faces stiff from the cold.

It always snowed for them at Christmas. And it would again this year. I just waited.

The day before Christmas Eve, the wind blew hard and the sky went gray as roof slates. We were glad to get indoors at teatime, draw the curtains, and pull up to the fire. And I felt a little glow of excitement inside me, like one of the hot coals.

When I woke in the night, I knew at once. Something was different about the light and the way the air smelled. The ceiling was silvery pale.

I went to the window. Oh, and it was so beautiful! The fat white snowflakes were tumbling softly out of the sky like feathers from a goose quilt, settling on the rooftops and the church tower and the fields all around. I hugged myself for joy. A white Christmas! Just as I'd known it would be.

In the morning, the whole world was different. A new country. A magic kingdom.

At eleven o'clock, Dad and I left the kitchen, full of the warm smells of baking, and went outside. It was very bright, and our breath smoked out on the air in plumes. I'd never seen the countryside look like this, softened and changed by the snow. And behind the low hills, the sky was gathering again, heavy with more to come. Our boots scrunched softly as we trudged along the path leading to the church. There, beside the path, we built our snowman. He was a really good big one by the time we were done, with a scarf and an old top hat. I thought we ought to give him a stocking to hang up too—he was one of the family now!

Later on, after lunch, we set off to fetch the Christmas tree and holly from the farm. On the way back, with the crows cawing around the bare trees and the lights going on in the houses, it was much colder, and it did start to snow again. Dad said if it went on like this we'd be cut off. Back home in the warmth again, we put up the tree and the green holly branches.

That night, Christmas Eve, the snow was the most beautiful of all; then Christmas suddenly seemed to be all around us in the air—you could almost feel it. The moon had come up, and we carried a lantern too; and when we began to sing the carols, people came to their windows and opened their doors to hear better and

Opposite: Painting by David Lenz. Image from Ideals Publications

welcome us; and I felt so happy and strangely sad at the same time. "In the Bleak Midwinter" had never seemed so true.

We went around the village, singing and being given mince pies and hot drinks. Everyone was so cheerful and friendly, and I hoped it would never end.

Quite suddenly, I was tired, and my head swam; a warm bed seemed a great place. But I wasn't too tired to hang up my stocking— or to stand at my window for a moment in the darkness, looking out at the night sky, the stars, and the moonlight on the pale snow.

After that, Christmas some- how became a great, happy blur of presents and people arriving and laughter, hot turkey, and roasting chestnuts and the crackling fire, and the snow was part of it all.

On Christmas afternoon and Boxing Day, everybody was out, and, on the slopes around, we

tobogganed: whooshing down and tumbling off into the snow and lugging the sleds back up to the top, over and over again. There was the sound of voices calling and laughing all around the fields; and then someone said the pond was frozen hard over, so we all went to see. People brought out skates, and there was the zip and the hiss of the blades across the ice and bright scarves and hats and new sweaters, as we whirled around and around in the late after- noon light.

And the whole time, I was remembering it to tell them when I was very old, just as people had always told me: *When we were young, they said, summers were long and hot, and it always snowed at Christmas. It doesn't happen nowadays,* they said. But it did. It snowed at Christmas that year. Just as I'd known it would.

Snow and Hearth

George Eliot

Snow lay on the croft and riverbank in undulations softer than the limbs of infancy; it lay with the neatliest finished border of every sloping roof, making the dark red gables stand out with a new depth of color; it weighed heavily on the laurels and fir trees, till it fell from them with a shuddering sound . . . there was no gleam, no shadow, for the heavens, too, were one still, pale cloud—no sound or motion in anything but the dark river that flowed and moaned like an unresting sorrow. But old Christmas smiled as he laid this cruel-seeming spell on the outdoor world, for he meant to light up home with a new brightness, to deepen all the richness of indoor color, and give a keener edge of delight to warm fragrance of food; he meant to prepare a sweet imprisonment that would strengthen the primitive fellowship of kindred, and make the sunshine of familiar human faces as welcome as the hidden daystar.

The merry Christmas,
    with its generous boards,
Its fire-lit hearths,
    and gifts and blazing trees,
Its pleasant voices uttering gentle words,
Its genial mirth, attuned to sweet accords,
Its holiest memories!
The fairest season of the passing year—
The merry, merry Christmas time is here.

—GEORGE ARNOLD

Photograph by Jessie Walker

Coming-Home Time
Virginia Blanck Moore

Christmas is coming-home time, near and far,
When wide-scattered families—wherever they are,
Wherever they've wandered, and far though they roam—
Feel in their hearts a hunger for home.

Each Yule decoration hung up on a street,
Each package-laden stranger they happen to meet,
Each scarlet-clad Santa in picture or store,
Renews the old longing to come home once more.

Each sound of sweet carols afloat in the night,
Each fir tree bedecked in its finery so bright,
Red Christmas tapers that flicker and burn,
Bid every wanderer's heart to return.

And come home they do, from far and from near,
To the folks and the scenes so familiar and dear,
Heeding the memories that beckon and call,
For Christmas is coming-home time for us all.

Joys of Christmas
Mary A. Barnard

The warmth of Christmas greetings
And the glow from Christmas cheer
Is enough to warm the hearts
And to last throughout the year;
For whate'er may be your plight
Or wherever you may roam,
There is nothing like Christmas
And the cozy warmth of home,
With loved ones all about you
And a chance to greet old friends.
These are pleasures Christmas brings
And a joy that knows no end.

CRYSTAL HILL © by Alex Krajewski. www.alexkrajewski.com

Going Home

The New York Times, December 25, 1948

The happiest holidays are those people "go home" for. Going home may mean youngsters returning from school or job, sometimes bringing their own younger youngsters with them. It may mean going to Grandma and Grandpa's. Home is where Father and Mother are, or where one of them was brought up. Home is a dreamland in which every effort is made to spoil children. Home is the fond memory held by parents of the days when they themselves were very young. Home is where the year's troubles and anxieties are forgotten. Home is where no unkind word is spoken, and where the good smells from the kitchen tell of deep affection. Home binds together the relatives by blood and the relatives by marriage and turns them into that most beautiful of human institutions—the family.

If trains are late or crowded, if planes can't get off, if Mother is worn out with packing and Father weary after his pre-holiday hours in the office, if many little things go wrong, who cares? When one is going home, a bit of hardship on the way makes the arrival a greater joy.

The tree is lighted and waiting. The old folks are at the door, their faces beaming with pure welcome. The day's mirth does not hide its tenderness. The laughter comes closer than that of other days to the laughter of the angels; the joke is on those who maintain that it does not come natural to human beings to love one another.

Many who are elderly today remember such holidays from long ago, when jingling sleigh bells were more familiar than automobile horns. Many who are now children will remember this day long years from now. The mechanisms of living change, the world changes, but the sweetness of family reunions, the bliss of "going home"—this abides.

Christmas and Grandmother's Kitchen
Rachel S. Fruh

No other place in all the world had the warmth and magic of Grandmother's kitchen at Christmastime. Every year on the first day of December, she tucked her plump anatomy into a wonderful red-checked apron, and this was the signal to the whole household that, for Grandmother at least, the holiday season had officially begun. Stalwart and spunky, she was the unrivaled monarch of her domain. With a smudge of flour on her chin and wisps of stray silver curling gently about her face, she moved purposely about the room, pulling crocks of sugar from the pantry, stoking the fire, and plunging her thick, strong fists into mounds of leavened dough.

Within a few hours, the plain little kitchen with its worn wooden floors and tired old furniture was transformed into a wonderland of childhood fancies. Even the eccentric old woodstove seemed to enjoy the excitement as it popped and spit contentedly in the corner, teasing the copper teakettle into singing tenor and steaming up the lace-framed windowpanes with its hot, smoky breath. On the front lid, thick chocolate syrup bubbled merrily in an iron kettle and spit out tiny beads that sizzled and danced on the stovetop. Next to it, a cauldron of nutty caramel fudge frothed and foamed to its peak of perfection. Meanwhile, inside the oven, another wonder was being performed. Out of its mysterious depths emerged giant cookie sheets laden with golden brown cutouts, popovers, and fat, saucy gingerbread boys bulging at the seams of their imaginary blue jeans. And across the room on the sideboard, a row of glass cookie jars proudly flaunted their holiday dainties: *Pfeffer Nüsse*, *Lebkuchen*, and sugar cookies the size of Grandmother's china saucers. Out of this happy clutter ascended a wondrous concoction, a fragrant intermingling of cinnamon, yeast sponge, lemon extract, melted butter, and fresh-ground cloves that intoxicated all who breathed it with the nostalgia of the holiday season.

Even though her red-checked apron has been folded and put away for the last time, the old woodstove has forever ceased to tease the copper teakettle into singing tenor, and the cookie jars are no longer filled, the memory of Grandmother and her kitchen will always warm my heart with the magic that is Christmas.

Photograph by Jessie Walker

Family Recipes

PINEAPPLE-STRAWBERRY CAKE

2   8-ounce packages cream cheese,
      softened
½   cup granulated sugar
1   teaspoon vanilla extract
3   eggs

1   package pineapple cake mix
1   cup water
1   16-ounce package frozen
      strawberries, thawed

Preheat oven to 350°F. In a large bowl, cream 1½ packages cream cheese until fluffy. Gradually add sugar, vanilla, and 1 egg. Beat well. Spread mixture evenly in a greased and lightly floured 9 x 13-inch pan. In a large bowl, combine cake mix, remaining cream cheese, 2 eggs, and water; beat 4 minutes. Spread over cheese mixture. Bake 40 to 50 minutes until a toothpick inserted in the middle comes out clean. Cool in pan 5 minutes. Remove from pan and cool completely. Serve topped with strawberries. Makes 12 servings.

CRUNCHY CUPS

1   pound white compound coating,
      wafers or pieces
1   cup crisp rice cereal
1   cup miniature marshmallows
½   cup broken pretzel pieces

1   cup granola cereal
1   cup roasted peanuts
50   candied cherry halves
50   pieces candied pineapple

Place compound coating in glass bowl; microwave on high 1 minute. Stir and microwave 1 minute more. Remove; stir to finish melting and blend in remaining ingredients except candied fruit. Spoon mixture into paper candy cups; garnish with pieces of candied cherries and pineapple. Makes 50 candies.

MIXED-UP FRUITCAKE COOKIES

1½ cups all-purpose flour	1 egg
1¼ teaspoons baking powder	¼ cup water
¼ teaspoon salt	¼ teaspoon brandy extract
1 teaspoon ground cinnamon	½ cup dried apricots, chopped
¼ teaspoon ground nutmeg	½ cup raisins
¼ teaspoon allspice	¼ cup mixed candied fruits
½ cup butter	½ cup chopped walnuts
1 cup granulated sugar	

Preheat oven to 400°F. In a medium bowl, sift together flour, baking powder, salt, and spices; set aside. In a large bowl, cream butter and sugar until light. Beat in egg, water, and brandy extract. Gradually add flour mixture.

Add fruits and nuts. Mix thoroughly. Drop by teaspoonfuls onto ungreased baking sheet. Bake 8 minutes or until lightly browned. Cool on rack. Makes 3 dozen cookies.

POINSETTIA COOKIES

3 cups all-purpose flour	½ teaspoon rum extract
1 teaspoon salt	1 cup shredded coconut
2 cups confectioners' sugar	1 cup butterscotch chips, divided
1 cup butter, softened	Granulated sugar
2 eggs	½ cup candied red cherries,
1 teaspoon vanilla extract	cut in wedges

Preheat oven to 375°F. In a medium bowl, sift together flour and salt; set aside. In a large bowl, beat together confectioners' sugar and butter. Add eggs and extracts and blend well. Mix in flour until well blended. Fold in coconut and ¾ cup of the butter-

scotch morsels. Chill dough until firm. Roll into 1-inch balls. Place on ungreased cookie sheets. Flatten cookie with bottom of glass dipped in granulated sugar. Place a butterscotch morsel in center of each cookie. Arrange cherry wedges in a circle around morsel to resemble a poinsettia. Bake about 12 minutes. Makes 5 dozen cookies.

from Let's Keep Christmas

Peter Marshall

Although your Christmas tree decorations will include many new gadgets, such as lights with bubbles in them . . . it's the old tree decorations that mean the most . . . the ones you save carefully from year to year . . . the crooked star that goes on the top of the tree . . . the ornaments that you've been so careful with.

And you'll bring out the tiny manger and the shed and the little figures of the Holy Family . . . and lovingly arrange them on the mantel or in the middle of the dining room table.

And getting the tree will be a family event, with great excitement for the children . . .

And there will be a closet into which you'll forbid your husband to look, and he will be moving through the house mysteriously with bundles under his coat, and you'll pretend not to notice . . .

There will be the fragrance of cookies baking, spices, and fruit cake . . . and the warmth of the house shall be melodious with the lilting strains of "Silent Night, Holy Night."

And you'll listen to the wonderful Christmas music on the radio. Some of the songs will be modern—good enough music perhaps—but it will be the old carols, the lovely old Christmas hymns, that will mean the most.

And forests of fir trees will march right into our living rooms . . . There will be bells on our doors and holly wreaths in our windows . . .

And we shall sweep the Noël skies for their brightest colors and festoon our homes with stars.

There will be a chubby stocking hung by the fireplace . . . and with finger to lip, you will whisper and ask your husband to tip-toe; for a little touseled head is asleep and must not be awakened until after Santa has come.

And finally Christmas morning will come. Don't worry—you'll be ready for it—you'll catch the spirit all right, *or it will catch you, which is even better.*

And then you will remember what Christmas means—the beginning of Christianity . . . the Second Chance for the world . . . the hope for peace . . . and the only way.

The promise that the angels sang is the most wonderful music the world has ever heard. "Peace on earth and goodwill toward men."

It was not a pronouncement upon the state of the world then, nor is it a reading of the international barometer of the present time . . . but it is a promise—God's promise—of what one day will come to pass.

The years that are gone are graveyards in which all the persuasions of men have crumbled into dust. If history has any voice, it is to say that all these ways of men lead nowhere. There remains one way—The Way—untried, untested,

Photograph by Jessie Walker

unexplored fully . . . the way of Him Who was born a Babe in Bethlehem.

In a world that seems not only to be changing, but even to be dissolving, there are some tens of millions of us who want Christmas to be the same . . . with the same old greeting, "Merry Christmas," and no other. We long for the abiding love among men of goodwill which the season brings . . . believing in this ancient miracle of Christmas with its softening, sweetening influence to tug at our heartstrings once again.

We want to hold on to the old customs and traditions because they strengthen our family ties, bind us to our friends, make us one with all mankind for whom the Child was born, and bring us back again to the God Who gave His only begotten Son, that "whosoever believeth in Him should not perish, but have everlasting life."

So we will not "spend" Christmas . . . nor "observe" Christmas. We will "keep" Christmas—keep it as it is . . . in all the loveliness of its ancient traditions.

May we keep it in our hearts, that we may be kept in its hope.

The Crèche

Carol Ryrie Brink

Gabriel had gathered moss,
Justine a tiny tree,
Francoise patted out the sand
Where Jean Baptiste could see.

They built the little stable up
And hung the golden star,
They set the tree
    and spread the moss
And viewed it from afar.

Their fingers trembled on the box
That held the holy things—
They took the Blessed Baby out
And dusted off the kings.

They made a little shining pool
From a looking glass;
Francoise placed
    the shepherd lads;
Justine, the weary ass.

Joseph and heaven-blue
    Mary fell
To eldest Gabriel—

The others crowded close to see
That he placed them well.

Between these two,
    the dimpled hands
Of little Jean Baptiste
Laid the smiling Jesus down—
The mightiest to the least.

When it was done
    they stood about
All silent in their places,
And years and years of
    seas dissolved before
The still light in their faces.

One said, "*Joli!*"
    and one said "*Bien!*"
A radience shone on them
As shone once on
    the shepherd lads
In far-off Behlehem.

HEAVEN IN MY HANDS *by Kathy Fincher (www.kathyfincher.com*

The Secret about Saint Joseph

Barb Neveu

There's a lump in my throat as I open the old cardboard box labeled, "Manger." I gently unwrap the first piece of the manger scene. It is Melchior. Reaching into the box I find Gaspar, two white sheep, the angel, and the Baby. Cradling the infant statue, my thoughts take flight to another Christmas some years ago.

"It's nearly time," called Mim, my grandmother. She motioned to the revered box on a table before her. Because Mim was the eldest of our family, it was her privilege to hand out the fragile, ceramic manger pieces to each of us. I had just turned seven, old enough to take an active part for the first time. I sat on the couch, close to Mim, and tried to guess who would get what piece. I had my favorites, like the blue and white angel who held the "Hallelujah" scroll; the blue-eyed donkey; and Saint Joseph, who carried a shiny lantern that swung back and forth. Mim would pass out the pieces one at a time, except for the Baby Jesus. It was Mim's honor to place him in the crib on Christmas morning.

My father had already set up the big manger on a table by the front window. It was a wonderful scene, compete with real straw on the roof and floor, and a music box in the loft that played "Silent Night." Aunt Annie was first, and she carefully unwrapped Balthasar. My mother uncovered my favorite angel, and my father got the two white sheep that were always wrapped up together. I started to squirm in my seat as pieces were handed to Aunt Lilly and Aunt Elaine. Mim finally handed me a newspaper-covered treasure.

When I discovered which one I had, my composure went down the drain, and I shrieked, "It's Joseph! I got Joseph!" I made a quick sweep around the room to plant a kiss on everyone's cheek. Then I placed Joseph in the straw, with his lantern facing out so I could see it. When Mary, the three kings, and all the animals were in place, my father wound the music box, and we sang with it on our way into the kitchen for a Christmas Eve feast. My bedtime arrived much too soon. But I had a plan.

Snuggled safe and warm in my bed, I dozed on and off, waiting until not a creature was stirring. Then I slid my feet into fuzzy slippers and sneaked into the parlor. I went directly to the manger and stood in awe at the sight before me. Joseph's lantern was ablaze with light. My stomach flip-flopped. Peering closer, I discovered it was a reflection of the streetlight on the lantern's silver foil. Not a miracle exactly, but I couldn't help reaching in for one more good look. Lifting Joseph carefully past the donkey and the cow, I nearly had him out when the lantern caught on some straw and I lost my grip. I pinched my eyes shut for an instant, and when I opened them again, I saw the statue teetering on the table's edge. I reached for it, but not quickly enough. Joseph fell to the floor. My heart stopped.

The shiny lantern, as well as Joseph's left hand, were missing. I checked the cuffs and creases of my pajamas, I looked in my slippers, I looked through the straw, then I got down on my hands and knees in the darkness to comb the floor. When I felt a sharp pain in my knee, I found the hand and the lantern. Grateful I hadn't crushed it, I took the broken statue back to my room. I sneaked into the kitchen to get some Elmer's glue, and back to my room. I didn't dare turn on a lamp, so I used what little light came in the window as I glued Joseph's hand back on. Then I heard a noise. Someone was up. I hopped under the covers pretending to be asleep. When everything was quiet again, I brought Joseph back to his place in the manger.

The next morning, I swept past the manger for a quick look. Joseph seemed fine to me. Later on, after we opened gifts, my father wound the music box in the manger. I realized I hadn't noticed earlier that the Baby Jesus was in the crib. But when had Mim put him there? This morning? During the night? Then I noticed Joseph, who didn't look right this time at all. Just as I was about to reach for him, Mim came up next to me and said, "Something doesn't look right. It seems off balance somehow."

I swallowed hard. In my most innocent voice I asked, "Do you think we should move the sheep?"

"No," she said, "it isn't the sheep." Then she looked me in the eyes and said, "I think it's Joseph."

Tears were so close my eyes burned, and just when I was about to confess that I had gotten up in the middle of the night, that Joseph and I had an accident, that I tried to fix it, and that in the

dark, I had glued his hand and the lantern back on, upside down, Mim smiled and said, "I think Joseph and Mary should trade places." She moved them so Joseph's broken hand was toward the back of the manger, and not noticeable unless you really looked.

"There, that's much better," she said. I threw my arms around her and hugged as hard as I could. I knew then that the secret would remain with Mim and me and Joseph.

Now, in my lap are the last two pieces of the manger to unwrap. One is the donkey with the blue eyes, the other is Joseph, still holding a lantern in his broken hand.

Christmas Carol

Henry Wadsworth Longfellow

When Christ was born in Bethlehem,
'Twas night, but seemed the noon of day;
The stars, whose light
Was pure and bright,
Shone with unwavering ray;
But one, one glorious star
Guided the Eastern Magi from afar.

Then peace was spread throughout the land;
The lion fed beside the tender lamb;
And with the kid,
To pastures led,
The spotted leopard fed;
In peace, the calf and bear,
The wolf and lamb reposed together there.

As shepherds watched their flocks by night,
An angel, brighter than the sun's own light,
Appeared in air,
And gently said,
"Fear not—be not afraid,
For lo! beneath your eyes,
Earth has become a smiling paradise."

The Animals That Night
Kathy L. May

We couldn't sleep, my aunt and I,
girl and child in the back-porch room,
so we wrapped ourselves in blankets
and slipped on shoes that clopped
    on the floor like hooves.

Outside we climbed the hill
toward stars,
bright eyes of animals
    crouching in the dark.

In the barn our flashlight blazed
on the cow, knee-deep in straw,
and the horse, who craned
    her neck to see us.

My aunt said,
The animals speak on Christmas Eve,
and I believed her
as we stood in the snuffling
dimness of the barn,
as we walked downhill past sheep bleating
something I almost understood,
back into our room
small and cool as a stall.

VI, 1988
Wendell Berry

Remembering that it happened once,
We cannot turn away the thought—
As we go out, cold, to our barns
Toward the long night's end—that we
ourselves are living in the world
It happened in when it first happened;
That we ourselves, opening a stall
(A latch thrown open countless times
Before), might find them breathing there,
Foreknown: the Child bedded in straw,
The mother kneeling over Him,
The husband standing in belief
He scarcely can believe, in light
That lights them from no source we see;
An April morning's light, the air
Around them joyful as a choir.
We stand with one hand on the door,
Looking into another world
That is this world, the pale daylight
Coming just as before, our chores
To do, the cattle all awake,
Our own white, frozen breath hanging
In front of us; and we are here
As we have never been before,
Sighted as not before, our place
Holy, although we knew it not.

Horse barn in the Methow Valley in Okanogan County, Washington.
Photograph by Mary Liz Austin/Austin Donnelly Photography

A Holy Birth

Matthew 1:18–25

Now the birth of Jesus Christ was on this wise: When as his mother Mary was espoused to Joseph, before they came together, she was found with child of the Holy Ghost.

Then Joseph her husband, being a just man, and not willing to make her a public example, was minded to put her away privily.

But while he thought on these things, behold, the angel of the Lord appeared unto him in a dream, saying, Joseph, thou son of David, fear not to take unto thee Mary thy wife: for that which is conceived in her is of the Holy Ghost.

And she shall bring forth a son, and thou shalt call his name JESUS: for he shall save his people from their sins.

Now all this was done, that it might be fulfilled which was spoken of the Lord by the prophet, saying,

Behold, a virgin shall be with child, and shall bring forth a son, and they shall call his name Emmanuel, which being interpreted is, God with us.

Then Joseph being raised from sleep did as the angel of the Lord had bidden him, and took unto him his wife:

And knew her not till she had brought forth her firstborn son: and he called his name JESUS.

Painting by George Hinke. Image from Ideals Publications

Shepherds and Angels

Luke 2:8–20

And there were in the same country shepherds abiding in the field, keeping watch over their flock by night.

And, lo, the angel of the Lord came upon them, and the glory of the Lord shone round about them: and they were sore afraid.

And the angel said unto them, Fear not: for, behold, I bring you good tidings of great joy, which shall be to all people.

For unto you is born this day in the city of David a Saviour, which is Christ the Lord.

And this shall be a sign unto you; Ye shall find the babe wrapped in swaddling clothes, lying in a manger.

And suddenly there was with the angel a multitude of the heavenly host praising God, and saying,

Glory to God in the highest, and on earth peace, good will toward men.

And it came to pass, as the angels were gone away from them into heaven, the shepherds said one to another, Let us now go even unto Bethlehem, and see this thing which is come to pass, which the Lord hath made known unto us.

And they came with haste, and found Mary, and Joseph, and the babe lying in a manger.

And when they had seen it, they made known abroad the saying which was told them concerning this child.

And all they that heard it wondered at those things which were told them by the shepherds.

But Mary kept all these things, and pondered them in her heart.

And the shepherds returned, glorifying and praising God for all the things that they had heard and seen, as it was told unto them.

Painting by George Hinke. Image from Ideals Publications

Worship of the Wise Men
Matthew 2:1–12

Now when Jesus was born in Bethlehem of Judaea in the days of Herod the king, behold, there came wise men from the east to Jerusalem,

Saying, Where is he that is born King of the Jews? for we have seen his star in the east, and are come to worship him.

When Herod the king had heard these things, he was troubled, and all Jerusalem with him.

And when he had gathered all the chief priests and scribes of the people together, he demanded of them where Christ should be born.

And they said unto him, In Bethlehem of Judaea: for thus it is written by the prophet,

And thou Bethlehem, in the land of Juda, art not the least among the princes of Juda: for out of thee shall come a Governor, that shall rule my people Israel.

Then Herod, when he had privily called the wise men, enquired of them diligently what time the star appeared.

And he sent them to Bethlehem, and said, Go and search diligently for the young child; and when ye have found him, bring me word again, that I may come and worship him also.

When they had heard the king, they departed; and, lo, the star, which they saw in the east, went before them, till it came and stood over where the young child was.

When they saw the star, they rejoiced with exceeding great joy.

And when they were come into the house, they saw the young child with Mary his mother, and fell down, and worshipped him: and when they had opened their treasures, they presented unto him gifts; gold, and frankincense and myrrh.

And being warned of God in a dream that they should not return to Herod, they departed into their own country another way.

Painting by George Hinke. Image from Ideals Publications

Christmas Carol

Paul Laurence Dunbar

Ring out, ye bells!
All Nature swells
With gladness of
   the wondrous story,
The world was lorn,
But Christ is born
To change our sadness
   into glory.

Sing, earthlings, sing!
Tonight a King
Hath come from heaven's
   high throne to bless us.
The outstretched hand
O'er all the land
Is raised in pity
   to caress us.

Come at His call;
Be joyful all;
Away with mourning
   and with sadness!
The heavenly choir
With holy fire
Their voices raise
   in songs of gladness.

The darkness breaks
And Dawn awakes,
Her cheeks suffused
   with youthful blushes.
The rocks and stones
In holy tones
Are singing sweeter
   than the thrushes.

Then why should we
In silence be,
When Nature lends
   her voice to praises;
When heaven and earth
Proclaim the truth
Of Him for whom
   that lone star blazes?

No, be not still,
But with a will
Strike all your harps
   and set them ringing;
On hill and heath
Let every breath
Throw all its power
   into singing!

Go tell it on the mountain,
Over the hills and everywhere;
Go tell it on the mountain,
That Jesus Christ is born.
—Author Unknown

San Juan Mountains, Colorado. Photograph by Dennis Frates

The Greatest Gift

Carol Round

"For God so loved the world that he gave his one and only Son, that whoever believes in him shall not perish but have eternal life" (John 3:16, NIV).

Can you imagine what it must have been like on that cold, starry night in Bethlehem? Mary and Joseph, alone, except for the animals whose home they had invaded in preparation for the birth of their child.

No modern-day birthing room or a luxury hotel. No heat. No electricity. No running water. No bed to rest their weary bodies as they awaited the birth of their child. No place for a small babe except a feeding trough for His cradle. However, it was from these humble beginnings that God gave us the greatest gift of all.

Christmas is a time to remember that gift, which, in reality, would become a sacrifice. With the advertising blitz and the glittery glitz of today's holiday season, how can we relate to that night more than two thousand years ago?

We must first remember the tiny package that was delivered into His mother's arms and wrapped in swaddling clothes. Good things do come in small packages.

In spite of all the modern-day toys with their bells and whistles, most children are content to play with the wrapping paper and bows. I have observed not only my sons' but also my grandchildren's fascination with simple things: a cardboard box, pots and pans, a wooden spoon, or an empty paper towel tube.

I can recall a discarded refrigerator box that my two sons confiscated. Over several months, the cardboard metamorphosed from a tunnel to a fort, then into a variety of other little boys' playthings before the pieces that remained were tossed in the trash.

I have listened to my parents tell stories of growing up during the Depression. My grandparents used their imagination to create toys from items that we, in today's society, would probably throw away.

A toy tractor made from a wooden spool, a sliver of soap, matches, and a rubber band provided hours of fun for my father and his brothers. They would race their new vehicles on the smooth wooden floors of their parents' home. Their homemade treasures were created from improvised items by parents who had to "make do" in a time when life was really less complicated.

Parents didn't have to worry about standing in long lines to fight for their chance to purchase a popular novelty item, stay up all night on Christmas Eve to assemble a toy, or race at the last minute to purchase batteries for a gift that would not walk or talk without them.

Mary and Joseph had to "make do" in their circumstances too. But it was from these humble beginnings that God gave us His Son, the greatest gift of all.

As you prepare to celebrate Christmas, avoid being consumed by the glamour of the season. Instead, remember that tiny baby who was born in simple surroundings.

What does this season mean to you? When you have received the greatest gift of all, the others pale in comparison.

Photograph by Dennis Frates

Our Best Christmas Gift
Victor Redick

They came across the desert;
They journeyed from afar;
They had no map or compass
To lead them to the star.

May that same star still
   bring us
To worship at His side
And give the love within us
To Him at Christmastide.

The splendor of the
   Christmas star
Filled the holy night;
It hovered over Bethlehem—
A beauteous, awesome sight!

It filtered in a window of
A little stable there

And touched the face of
   Mary's Son,
The Babe beyond compare.

It guided shepherds to
   His side;
They knelt in wonderment
Before the tiny King of kings,
God given, heaven-sent.

The eyes of faith can
   see it still,
Shining through the years . . .
Drawing hearts and
   souls to Him
Who banishes all fears.

LOVING FATHER, HELP US REMEMBER the birth of Jesus, that we may share in the song of the angels, the gladness of the shepherds, and the worship of the wise men.

Close the door of hate, and open the door of love all over the world.

Let kindness come with every gift, and good desires with every greeting.

Deliver us from evil by the blessing which Christ brings, and teach us to be merry with clear hearts.

May the Christmas morning make us happy to be Thy children, and the Christmas evening bring us to our beds with grateful thoughts, forgiving and forgiven, for Jesus' sake. Amen!

—Robert Louis Stevenson

Christmas lights reflected in Lake Winnipesaukee,
Meredith, New Hampshire. Photograph by William H. Johnson

Christmas

Oliver Murray Edwards

'Tis Christmas Day! 'Tis Christmas Day!
    With joy the church bells ring.
'Tis Christmas Day! 'Tis Christmas Day!
    The birthday of our King.
Our richest gifts are loving hearts,
    So hearts of love we bring.
With deeds and gifts we voice our love
    And Christmas carols sing.

'Tis Christmas Day! 'Tis Christmas Day!
    And children's joy is ours
As memory turns back the page
    To childhood's early hours.
For Jesus too was once a child
    And shares in children's joy;
'Tis in the giving that we find
    Love pure without alloy.

'Twas Christmas Day! First Christmas Day!
    In years long, long ago,
In Bethlehem a child was born
    In stable manger low;
The baby King, the infant Christ,
    Received first Christmas cheer
From wise men kneeling on the floor
    With shepherds standing near.

And ever since that Christmas Day
    With joy the church bells ring
And loudly peal the shouts of joy
    In honor of the King.
And rich the gifts of loving hearts
    Each Christmas Day doth bring;
With deeds and gifts we voice our love
    And Christmas carols sing.

Sunrise over church in Exeter, New Hampshire.
Photograph © Photographers Choice RF/SuperStock

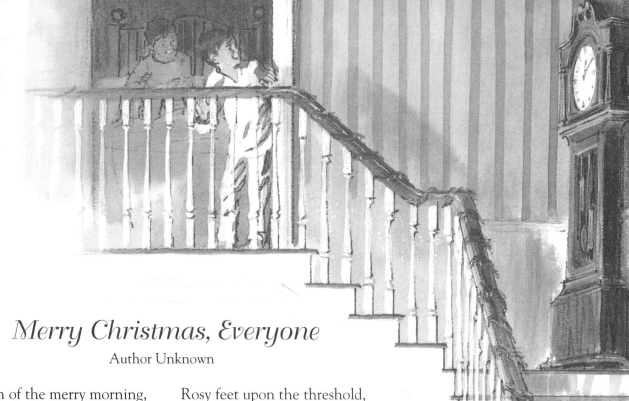

Merry Christmas, Everyone

Author Unknown

In the rush of the merry morning,
When the red burns through
   the gray,
And the wintry world lies waiting
For the glory of the day;
Then we hear a fitful rushing
Just without upon the stair,
See two white phantoms coming,
Catch the gleam of sunny hair.

Are they Christmas fairies stealing
Rows of little socks to fill?
Are they angels floating hither
With their message of goodwill?
What sweet spell are these
   elves weaving,
As like larks they chirp and sing?
Are these palms of peace
   from heaven
That these lovely spirits bring?

Rosy feet upon the threshold,
Eager faces peeping through,
With the first red ray of sunshine,
Chanting cherubs come in view;
Mistletoe and gleaming holly,
Symbols of a blessed day,
In their chubby hands they carry,
Streaming all along the way.

Well we know them,
   never weary
Of this innocent surprise;
Waiting, watching, listening
   always
With full hearts and tender eyes,
While our little household angels,
White and golden in the sun,
Greet us with the sweet
   old welcome—
"Merry Christmas, everyone!"

Photograph by William H. Johnson

Gift Exchanges

Henry Van Dyke

The custom of exchanging presents on a certain day in the year is very much older than Christmas and means very much less. It has obtained in almost all ages of the world and among many different nations. It is a fine thing or a foolish thing as the case may be; an encouragement to friendliness or a tribute to fashion; an expression of good nature or a bid for favor; an outgoing of generosity or a disguise of greed; a cheerful old custom or a futile old farce according to the spirit which animates it and the form which it takes.

But when this ancient and variously interpreted tradition of a day of gifts was transferred to the Christmas season, it was brought into vital contact with an idea which must transform it, and with an example which must lift it up to a higher plane. The example is the life of Jesus. The idea is unselfish interest in the happiness of others.

The great gift of Jesus to the world was Himself. He lived with and for men. He kept back nothing. In every particular and personal gift that He made to certain people there was something of Himself that made it precious. . . .

When He gave bread and fish to the hungry multitude who had followed Him out among the hills by the Lake of Gennesaret, the people were refreshed and strengthened by the sense of the personal care of Jesus for their welfare, as much as by the food which He bestowed upon them. It was another illustration of the sweetness of "a dinner of herbs where love is."

The gifts of healing which He conferred upon many different kinds of sufferers were in every case evidences that Jesus was willing to give something of Himself—His thought, His sympathy, His vital power—to the men and women among whom He lived. Once, when a paralytic was brought to Jesus on a bed, He surprised everybody, and offended many, by giving the poor wretch the pardon of His sins before He gave new life to his body. That was just because Jesus thought before He gave; because He desired to satisfy the deepest need; because, in fact, He gave something of Himself in every gift. All true Christmas giving ought to be after this pattern.

Not that it must all be solemn and serious. For the most part it deals with little wants, little joys, little tokens of friendly feeling. But the feeling must be more than the token, else the gift does not really belong to Christmas.

It takes time and effort and unselfish expenditure of strength to make gifts in this way. But it is the only way that fits the season. The finest Christmas gift is not the one that costs the most money but the one that carries the most love.

But how seldom Christmas comes—only once a year; and how soon it is over—a night and a day! If that is the whole of it, it seems not much more durable than the little toys that one buys on the street-corner. They run for an hour and then the spring breaks and the legs come off and nothing remains but a contribution to the dust heap.

But surely that need not and ought not to be the whole of Christmas—only a single day of generosity ransomed from the dull servitude of a selfish year—only a single night of merrymaking

Photograph by Steven Randazzo/SuperStock

celebrated in the slave-quarters of a selfish race! If every gift is the token of a personal thought, a friendly feeling, an unselfish interest in the joy of others, then the thought, the feeling, the interest may remain after the gift is made.

The little present or the rare and long-wished-for gift (it matters not whether the vessel be of gold or silver or iron or wood or clay, or just a small bit of birch bark folded into a cup) may carry a message something like this:

I am thinking of you today, because it is Christmas, and I wish you happiness. And tomorrow, because it will be the day after Christmas, I shall still wish you happiness; and so on, clear through the year. I may not be able to tell you about it every day because I may be far away, or because both of us may be very busy, or perhaps because I cannot even afford to pay the postage on so many letters or find the time to write them. But that makes no difference. The thought and the wish will be here just the same. In my work and in the business of life, I mean to try not to be unfair to you or injure you in any way. In my pleasure, if we can be together I would like to share the fun with you. Whatever joy or success comes to you will make me glad. Without pretense and in plain words, goodwill to you is what I mean, in the spirit of Christmas.

It is not necessary to put a message like this into high-flown language, to swear absolute devotion and deathless consecration. In love and friendship, small, steady payments on a gold basis are better than immense promissory notes. Nor, indeed, is it always necessary to put the message into words at all, nor even to convey it by a tangible token. To feel it and to act it out— that is the main thing.

There are a great many people in the world whom we know more or less, but to whom for various reasons we cannot very well send a Christmas gift. But there is hardly one in all the circles of our acquaintance with whom we may not exchange the touch of Christmas life.

In the outer circles, cheerful greetings, courtesy, consideration; in the inner circles, sympathetic interest, hearty congratulations, honest encouragement; in the inmost circle, comradeship, helpfulness, tenderness—*"Beautiful friend tried by sun and wind/Durable from the daily dust of life."*

After all, Christmas living is the best kind of Christmas giving.

Featured Poet

Christmas Kindness

Eileen Spinelli

Stirrers of soup,
share bread
and bowls
and grace.

Quarrelers, hush
in starry dark
embrace.

Painters of words,
paint LOVE
on crumbling walls.

Singers of song,
lift joy
in lonely halls.

Makers of quilts,
stitch warmth
into the chill.

Breakers of news,
bring stories
of goodwill.

Swingers of lanterns,
throw light
against the gloom.

Keepers of inns,
unlatch your hearts,
make room.

Painting by Jay Killian. Image from Ideals Publications

THROUGH MY WINDOW

Christmas Changes

Pamela Kennedy

The cold December wind lashed sleet against the windshield. My daughter had just picked me up at the airport in Seattle, and we were driving the sixty miles to our beach house at Hood Canal to prepare for a belated family Christmas. I didn't feel particularly celebratory. My mind wandered back six months:

My husband and I sat on the sunny deck of our newly finished beach house, sipping iced tea and feeling contented. I reached for the day's mail and ripped open an envelope from our son.

"Oh, no!" I wailed. "He won't be able to make it home to Hawaii for Christmas this year! At his new job he gets New Year's off, but not Christmas."

"You know, I've been thinking," said my husband. "I don't think we can count on your mom making the trip this year either, and if Anne gets cast in that play she's auditioning for, the run extends until December 30."

Circumstances seemed to be conspiring to destroy our traditional family celebration. I wasn't averse to most changes—during twenty-eight years in the Navy we had moved eighteen times! But I clung tenaciously to our holiday customs. We were always together on December 25; the tree was always decorated the same way; Christmas morning we always followed the same routine. In our ever-changing lives, I had counted on that one thing to remain constant.

My husband took my hand. "Maybe we could start some new traditions."

"I am not interested in new traditions . . . isn't that an oxymoron anyway?" I got up, went inside, and banged around in the kitchen fixing dinner.

Wise man that he is, my husband stayed outside for a while. Later that night, as we lay in bed he said, "OK, how about this? We fly here for Christmas after Christmas?"

"What?"

"We fly here and celebrate on New Year's Day. Everyone can be here—we just pretend it's Christmas."

"What about the tree? What about the decorations? What about getting the place ready and cooking and everything?"

"OK, you fly back a few days early and get everything set up. It could work." His voice sounded tentative. "It would be different, but at least we'd all be together."

"I don't know." I realized I was acting like a spoiled child, pouting because she couldn't get her way. Something in my heart didn't want to embrace one more change, to see the children grown up and our parents grown old, to admit that we, too, were moving towards a new stage in our lives. I sighed and rolled over, ending the discussion.

In the morning, we avoided Christmas talk. Friends were expected, and I needed to dash to town for a picnic tablecloth. On the way, I stopped at the thrift store, thinking I might find a gently used one and save a few dollars in the process. As luck would have it, I discovered a brightly striped cloth that was just perfect. I paid and headed for the door, almost colliding with a clerk carrying an artificial Christmas tree. She apologized, setting the tree in the front window. It was six feet tall, and narrow. I walked out, then turned around, squinting at the skinny tree. A white price tag dangled from a branch—a single, sad ornament swinging in the summer breeze. Tears sprang to my eyes. I stalked back into the Nifty Thrifty, slapped down a ten-dollar bill, and said, "I'm taking the tree." I grabbed the artificial evergreen, tossed it in the car, and drove back to the cabin.

"Here's the tablecloth, and there's a Christmas tree in the back," I said to my husband. "And don't ask." He didn't.

We returned to Hawaii, made holiday travel plans, and celebrated a quiet Christmas together. Now here I was, on a cold, stormy late December night, heading for our belated family celebration.

"I don't see much holiday cheer out there," I offered, staring at the wet highway.

"Well, we do have the Nifty Thrifty tree," Anne offered, and I sighed thinking of the naked little artificial fir awaiting us at the beach house.

As we turned down the dark driveway, our headlights illuminated a Christmas wreath on the front door. "Where did that come from?"

"Maybe the neighbor put it there," Anne offered, parking the car.

We grabbed our grocery bags, unlocked the door, and flipped on the lights. I gasped. The house was filled with red candles nestled in holly. Fragrant garlands topped the windows, and on a bed of spun angel's hair, a beautiful Nativity scene sparkled under a dusting of artificial snow. My daughter laughed and beckoned me upstairs. She ran ahead, and when I entered the living room our skinny little second-hand tree glistened with tiny colored lights, shiny red balls, and sparkling gold stars.

"Merry Christmas, Mom!" she said, giggling at my astonishment. "I wanted to surprise you so I came down here last weekend! After all those years you and Daddy did everything for us, it's fun to turn the tables. I just wanted you to know that it's OK if Christmas changes."

Opening my arms, I welcomed my daughter into my embrace. Over her shoulder I glimpsed the tree and smiled. It seemed to shine even brighter through a mist of thankful tears.

Bits & Pieces

May you have the gladness of Christmas,
Which is hope;
The spirit of Christmas,
Which is peace;
The heart of Christmas,
Which is love.
—*Ada V. Hendricks*

A bright and blessed Christmas Day,
With echoes of the angels' song,
And peace that cannot pass away,
And holy gladness, calm and strong,
And sweet heart carols, flowing free!
This is my Christmas wish to thee!
—*Frances Ridley Havergal*

Love came down at Christmas,
Love all lovely, Love Divine;
Love was born at Christmas,
Stars and angels gave the sign.
—*Christina G. Rossetti*

Blessed by the Christmas sunshine, our natures,
perhaps long leafless, bring forth new love, new
kindness, new mercy, new compassion.

—Helen Keller

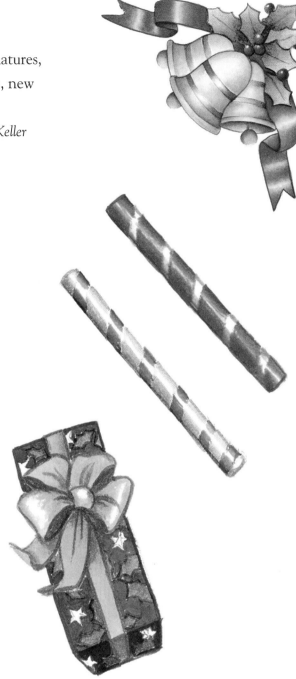

It is Christmas in the mansion,
Yule-log fires and silken frocks;
It is Christmas in the cottage,
Mother's filling little socks.
It is Christmas on the highway
In the thronging, busy mart;
But the dearest, truest Christmas
Is the Christmas in the heart.

—Author Unknown

Christmas, my child, is love in action. . . .
When you love someone, you give to them, as
God gives to us. The greatest gift He ever gave
was the Person of His Son, sent to us in
human form so that we might know what God
the Father is really like! Every time we love,
every time we give, it's Christmas.

—Dale Evans Rogers

As fits the holy Christmas birth,
Be this, good friends, our carol still—
Be peace on earth, be peace on earth,
To men of gentle will.

—William Makepeace Thackeray

Christmas Thoughts

J. C. Penney

How intangible and indescribable is the spirit of Christmas! It is something far deeper than mere gift-giving and all the spontaneous joy and gaiety that goes with the season. It expresses itself in the very spirit with which it draws people together. It weaves itself into a golden cord that binds us all into a spirit that has been called for centuries "goodwill toward men." The story of the Babe in the manger, the star of Bethlehem, the three wise men is old but ever new. One cannot think of it without being struck with the rare beauty and simplicity of it all. Yet there is a tendency to overlook the deep religious significance of Christ's birth. Christmas is not just a time for festivity and merrymaking. It is more than that. It is a time for the contemplation of eternal things. The Christmas spirit is a spirit of giving and forgiving. How can we expect our children to know and experience the joy of giving unless we teach them that the greater pleasure in life lies in the art of giving rather than receiving? We cannot very well tell the art of giving unless we practice it. But to give with the thought of getting will not help matters, for then giving becomes a matter of bookkeeping. We should make the Yuletide season an occasion not merely for the giving of material things but an occasion for the giving of that which counts infinitely more—the giving of self. We are our brother's keeper. Let us keep this truth in mind. Let us ever extend peace and goodwill to men.

Photograph by Steve Terrill

Ring On, O Happy Bells

Joy Belle Burgess

Ring on, O bells of gladness,
With your message of good cheer;
Peal forth the merry tidings
In cadence sweet and clear.

Chime forth your skyborne music,
With its intervals of mirth,

Arouse the aspirations
And hopes of all the earth.

Ring on, O bells of gladness,
With the joy you now impart;
Ring on and on, O happy bells,
And bring a song to every heart.

ISBN-13: 978-0-8249-1316-8

Published by Ideals Publications, a Guideposts Company
535 Metroplex Drive, Suite 250, Nashville, Tennessee 37211
www.idealsbooks.com

Publisher, Peggy Schaefer
Editor, Melinda Rathjen
Copy Editor, Kaye Dacus
Designer, Marisa Jackson
Permissions Editor, Patsy Jay

Cover: Photograph by Nancy Matthews
Inside front cover: Painting by Ray App. Image from Ideals Publications
Inside back cover: Painting by Ray App. Image from Ideals Publications

ACKNOWLEDGMENTS:

BERRY, WENDELL. "Our Christmas Tree" and "VI, 1988" from *A Timbered Choir: The Sabbath Poems 1979–1997* by Wendell Berry, Published by Counterpoint Press, Perseus Books. BRINK, CAROL RYRIE. "The Crèche" from *Commonweal* magazine. CLARK, BILLY C. "My Mother's Christmas Tree" by Billy C. Clark, from *A Kentucky Christmas*, University of Kentucky Press. Used by permission of the author. EDWARDS, OLIVER MURRAY. "Christmas" from *From the Depths* by Oliver Murray Edwards, copyright © 1928. Revilo Press. FIELD, RACHEL. "For Christmas" from *Poems* by Rachel Field. Macmillan Publishing Company, NY, 1957. Used by permission of Simon & Schuster Books for Young Readers, an imprint of Simon & Schuster. FISHER, AILEEN. "December" from *Do Rabbits Have Christmas?* by Aileen Fisher. Copyright © 2007 by Boulder Public Library Foundation, Inc. First used in *That's Why* by Nelson, NY, 1946. Reprinted by permission of Henry Holt and Company. HILL, SUSAN. "White Christmas." Copyright © 1990 by Susan Hill. Commissioned by the *Royal Mail* and reprinted in *The Christmas Collection* by Susan Hill, published by Candlewick Press, 1994. MARSHALL, PETER. Excerpt from *Let's Keep Christmas* by Peter Marshall. Copyright © 1952, 1953 by Catherine Marshall. Used by permission of Baker Publishing Group. NEW YORK TIMES. "Going Home" originally titled "Home for the Holidays" from *The New York Times*, Dec. 25, 1948. Used by permission of the New York Times Agency. PETERS, FRITZ. "The Family Will Come," an excerpt from "December–The Tree," from *The Book of the Year* by Fritz Peters. Published by Harper Children's Books, 1950. ROUND, CAROL. "The Greatest Gift," an excerpt from *CAPPER'S* magazine, Dec. 2006. Ogden Publications Inc. OUR SINCERE THANKS to the following authors or their heirs, some of whom we may have been unable to locate: Mary A. Barnard, D. R. Barnes, Nora M. Bozeman, Rachel S. Fruh, Carol Bessent Hayman, Pamela Kennedy, Kathy L. May, Virginia Blanck Moore, Barb Neveu, J. C. Penney, Lolita Pinney, Victor Redick, Eileen Spinelli, Harriet Whipple. Every effort has been made to establish ownership and use of each selection in this book. If contacted, the publisher will be pleased to rectify any inadvertent errors or omissions in subsequent reprints.